Love Language

ISBN 978-3-033-10391-7

m. lovehall

introduction

my interpretation and understanding
of "love language" is ways to articulate love.

this collection introduces my love language.

this is how i love.

i didn't restrict myself to only put poetry
into this collection but combined it with
short prose and quotes, since the intention
of this book was to express love
in whatever way it wanted to be expressed.

while i didn't write the following compositions
out of love for myself, i find it very important
to point out that you don't need anyone's love
to feel complete except yours.

all the love you desire to feel
is already inside you.

at all times.

contents

to the strongest woman i know.
to the person i admire to see grow.
to the one my love i will always show.

you're the brightest light i've ever seen.

seed

i spent years working
on myself by myself.

i got my own peace,
joy and happiness.

i'm not going to rob yours.

- a promise

STEALING GLANCES

i stopped chasing after girls
once i stole a glance at you.

the urge disappeared
once you appeared.

starstruck.
you had me speechless.

somehow i still managed
to put some words together.

you gave me the cutest smile
and i knew we'd end up together.

a thief.

the way
you're stealing
everyone's attention

and keeping
mine hostage.

i tried to steal your heart
but you caught me.

you still fell for me
but i caught you.

- partners in crime

forget texting.

i'll be at your door
with flowers and food
on a thursday evening.

what's up?

you can take
your time
trusting me.

i'm in no rush.

i have no
hidden agenda.

i know some sunsets
i want to introduce you to.

- date

SEASONS (PART I)

summer is my chance to

take you out
&
get to know you.

as the sun sets late
and the days are long

we can simply go for a ride
and vibe out to your favorite song.

you're like 90s r&b tunes.

they just don't
make them

like you no more.

i hadn't even met you
and yet it was you

i was looking for
in everyone else.

12

i'm stargazing but i'm looking at you.

i get lost
looking into your eyes

but deep down i know
i've finally been found.

forget everything
you know about love

and let my appreciation
for you define it again.

i look at you and see
nothing that needs to be fixed

but everything that needs to be loved.

i'll show you the world in a bit.
let me show you the universe first.

let's start within.

FROM WITHIN

i want you to see how
wonderful love can be.

how healing my heart
for yours can be.

how my soul
can set yours free.

i want you to see that
love starts from within

and only then your
life can truly begin.

i can give you
my word and my heart.

that's my offer.
that's my promise.

that's all i've got.

i honor you by not comparing you.

THE "5 LOVE LANGUAGES"

First week
i walked you home.

Second week
i surprised you with flowers.

Third week
i took you out on a date
and we talked for hours.

Fourth week
i stayed up late and
wrote you a love letter.

Fifth week
you asked me to hold you and
thanked me for making you feel better.

arms wide open.
here to keep you safe.

no words required.
hugs are love unspoken.

when
our
bodies
touch

stars align.

23

your skin complexion is my favorite color.

EFFORT

your past i cannot change.
your future i will affect.

your presence i'm here for.
your peace i will protect.

your time is what i ask for.
your attention i will never neglect.

your affection i try to mirror.
your love i promise i will reflect.

the only thing
on my bucket list

is to check off yours.

- genie

you told me
you love
the way i think.

with you
on my mind
most of the time

i'd be surprised
if someone wouldn't.

you never get tired
of my love letters.

you collected them all
even asked for more.

got me thinking that
somewhere somehow

i've loved you before.

- past life lovers

28

the growth of
my capacity
to love
didn't stop
when i met you.

it started there.

DIVINITY

i don't ever want to take
my eyes off you again.

your beauty is appealing, sure
but there's much more to you.

it's your soul i see, it's pure.

you're the embodiment of love
sent directly from the source above.

i'll always be more
than a friend to you.

consider me a soul you
can always come talk to.

any day any time.
on good or bad terms.

i'll always be there for you.

a scarred heart doesn't scare me away.

in fact,
it shows me exactly how to love you.

32

words are just words.

i insist that
you look
for my love
in my actions.

i won't ever need
second chances
when it comes to you.

that's how you know
how sure i am of you.

34

you are a mystery
yet you have nothing to hide.

what a beautiful confusion.

11:11

but you're mine already.

36

i'm not the best photographer

but i can picture us
growing old together *perfectly*.

STORAGE (PART I)

i want to make sure that before
one of us leaves this earth

i showed you all the love
i have stored for you

and we better get started 'cause
it's going to take a few decades.

it's up to us to create the
love we want to experience.

let's unite our minds and
work out this plan together.

these feelings
i have for you
will cause me
to do miracles
for you.

watch me.

soil

embrace your past.
it has brought you to me.
every step was necessary.

i embrace my past.
every step was necessary.
it has brought me to you.

43

my life peaked when you
confessed your love for me

and it hasn't declined since.

44

THE PLOT

you letting me love you turned out
to be the best decision you've ever made.

i could've told you that
the first time we met

but just like me showing
you my favorite movies

i never spoil the plot
if you don't get it yet.

i rather sit back with a smile and
watch you figure it out on your own.

45

my skin care routine consists of your kisses.

TAGGED

i'm scrolling through my thoughts.
my timeline is made out of you.

you're the topic that keeps trending.
you're the trend that's never ending.

you're the highlight of my story.
you're the key to my success and glory.

my instincts tell me to only follow you
so every heartbeat i dedicate to you.

i make sure that whenever
i get better at loving myself

i get better at loving you too.

i am

your shoulder
to lean on

your arms
to fall into

your hand
to hold

your fingers
to count on.

trust me
i got you.

i love you as a whole.
flaws *and* imperfections.

wrap it all up.
i want all of you.

anyone who would've
got you would've won.

anyone who would've
got me would've won.

only right we got each other.

we both deserve the world.

let's make sure we both
give it to ourselves first

so we don't feel the pressure
of giving it to each other.

52

my life right now is
all about love and art.

in other words
all about you and you.

VULNERABILITY

opening up to you is easy.

you don't judge.
you don't interrupt.

you just listen.

you don't assume.
you don't wander.

you just listen.

you're present
and i can feel it.

my heart's wounded
but you help me heal it.

54

i admire you for
the person you **are**.

not *were* or *will be*.

- now

55

you are
the type
you have to
ask god for

to receive.

i know i should strive to
become better for myself

but half of the times
i'm working on me for you.

so thank you for inspiring me
to outgrow my own obstacles.

whoever it ends up benefiting.

it's not "as long as we got each other"

it's "as long as we both got ourselves"

that we can fully be here for one another.

NEVER LEAVING

you stay away from drama.
you don't let it get to you.

you don't seek attention
but you are the attraction.

so naturally people will
always be drawn to you.

like tourists most of them will
only come just to leave again

but i'm here to stay and
make you believe again;

you're a home to me and
every single atom inside of me.

you defined home.

for once and for all.

BEAUTY (PART I)

the way your eyes
match your hair.

the way your hair
matches your skin.

the way your skin
matches your eyes.

the way you always
have me mesmerized.

you are a star to me.

it's only a matter of time
till the world catches up.

i got a heart full of love for you.

63

SUNDAY MORNING

in your underwear
with your messy hair
on a sunday morning.

you're unaware
of how perfect you look
when you're not even trying.

don't mind if i stare
you look like an angel
it's not even worth denying.

you didn't only check
every criteria off my list,

you added more to it.

you're so much more than
i could've ever asked for.

65

we're so in tune
with each other

our egos are
third wheeling.

66

talk to me.

anytime.
anywhere.
about anything.

i'm available
for you always.

67

you're a never ending sunset.

68

she doesn't speak *from* the heart.

she *is* the heart.

she speaks *as* the heart.

POINT OF VIEW

seeing yourself from
my pov is a privilege
you won't ever have

so allow me to tell you
all about yourself from
angles you can't see

and make you realize
that you are as perfect as
a woman can possibly be.

you,
my ideas
and the universe

are things i could talk
about all day everyday.

71

it's me and you
against the world.

not by chance
but by choice.

we are all we need.

it feels like
we're just
an old couple
with old souls
reincarnated in
young bodies.

looks like our
past life wish
came true.

AS YOU ARE

i consider you to be perfect
even though nobody's flawless.

not me, not you.

my definition of perfect
is something so beautiful

you wouldn't dare to change it.

i want you to come to me as you are.

i love consciously.
i *choose* to love you.

it's not a spell i'm under.
it's a decision i make every day.

willingly and wholeheartedly
with absolutely no regrets.

by having the ability to walk
away and *promising* you to stay

i present to you my
ultimate commitment.

75

it's not that

i can't get mad at you.
i just choose not to.

i don't raise my voice.
i raise my vibration.

i treat you intentionally.
i love you mindfully.

TAKING PICTURES

i can't stop taking pictures of you
my phone is running out of storage.

the way you pose,
unintentional yet so appealing.

in your clothes
yet so revealing.

your intentions are clear
my doubts nonexistent.

even when you're near
even when you're distant

you always keep it real
you're always consistent.

allow me to take one more picture
allow me to remind you one more time

the most beautiful image of you
is the one i keep to myself;

it's the way i perceive you
it's the way i see you.

if you could
enter my mind

all you would
see are mirrors.

loving life & living love.

you gave life a new meaning.
you gave love a new meaning.

WIFE

i can't help but think of you when
i stare into the open night sky.

so many stars but
only one gives us life.

so many people but
i just want you as my wife.

a shooting star just passed by
and there goes my only wish.

water

some people
ask me how
i can be so
sure of you.

i say 'cause
i never had
to question it.

83

the realest thing
i ever wrote was

my name next to yours.

84

we lose together.
we win together.

we hurt together.
we heal together.

we fall together.
we rise together.

85

i asked my
guardian angels

to look after you too.

- prayers

SEASONS (PART II)

winter is my excuse to

keep you closer
&
hold you tighter.

as the weather's getting colder
and the days are getting shorter

you can simply seek my heart for shelter.

you get nothing
but the best from me

'cause you're nothing
but the best for me.

88

if you could see yourself through my eyes

you would never doubt yourself again.

- the universe

89

i'll accuse you
of being beautiful

until you plead guilty.

you are the inspiration
for every form
of expression
of love
of mine.

91

whatever life
throws at me

whatever
chances i get

they're not
worth
considering

if it results in
sacrificing you.

let's not forget
that you're the
opportunity of
a lifetime here.

BEAUTY (PART II)

you have been made
with such perfection.

eyes, hair, lips.
thighs, back, hips.

skin, height, physique.
you are literally beauty

at its peak.

93

before ***anything***,
you're my friend.

the best i ever had.

94

you save me.
i save you.

no victims.
we both heroes.

ANGEL

let me take off the weight
that's been pulling you down.

let me show you
that you can fly.

let me prove to you
that you've been
an angel all along

and even though you're
here with me right now

heaven is where you truly belong.

to my future daughter,

i got you the best mom possible.

there's not a thing
i wouldn't do for you

and yet there's so
little you ask me for.

this only makes me want to
give you the world even more.

you're living life as if it
was a dance you've been
practicing an eternity for.

it's a pleasure
being able to share
this dance floor with you.

i will always love you
but i'm not quoting whitney.

because i don't just
wanna dance with *somebody*.

i only wanna dance with **you**.

WILD THOUGHTS

despite my love for music
i still rather listen to you.

despite my love for movies
i still rather look at you.

despite my love for food
...

you know where i'm going with this.

my love story is special

because you're in it.

i see you constantly
working on yourself.

i don't care how fast
you're progressing.

i celebrate you trying.

i keep you in my arms.
i keep you in my prayers.

you're protected in the physical.
you're protected in the spiritual.

every time you find yourself
scared or in fear

remember that you got me
i'm always here.

a safe place where you can
comfortably shed a tear.

THE JOURNEY

life's a play.
love's a game.

promised to play it
but never each other.

i know we already won
'cause we got one another.

everything that's yet to come
is nothing else but a celebration

'cause we both know that the
journey is the true destination.

i don't fear losing you
as much as i fear
you losing yourself.

the world needs you
more than i want you.

don't ever let me or
someone else change
the core of who you are.

the word "love"
has lost its meaning
throughout this generation.

i call what we have nature.

i don't love you based on
the way you love me.

*i love you regardless
of how you love me.*

the love you share for me
makes this relationship
a beautiful place to be in

but it has nothing to do with
why or *how much* i love you.

- unconditional love

deep, real, honest, genuine
and most importantly *needed*.

conversations with you are like no others.

SOULMATES

i'm not even sure if i believe
in the idea of soulmates

but if i did

there's no question
as to who it *would be.*

you're my heart's desire.
you're my soul's longing.

if not you
i don't know who *could be.*

i look at you and
recognize myself.

i see
the whole
universe
lying
within you.

- enlightenment

i love
who i am

and i love
who you

are helping
me become.

- growth and evolution

113

TREASURE

down to earth.
wings attached.

you could fly.
heaven sent.

heart of gold.
treasure found.

digging deep.
my love for you

is so profound.

pouring my heart
out to you feels like

my cup is being filled too.

- healthy love

i love your commitment to

inner healing and self love.

my love

for

my love.

- fair trade

you don't even know
how much you inspire me

by simply being yourself.

DIVINE FEMININE

as if being able to
grow life inside you
wasn't enough
evidence to prove

the most important
contributor
to life before
anyone else are you.

to protect and provide
is a small price to pay
compared to the pain
you have to go through

because none of us
would be breathing
if it wasn't for the gift
that was entrusted in you.

sometimes
all i can do
is sit back and
watch you be you.

it's beautiful.
you're beautiful.

sunlight

when i think of love i think of you.

after all these years

you are still
the first thought
i have every morning.

for you

i would've waited forever.

STORAGE (PART II)

it's impossible for
me to run out of
love to give to you.

i've stored the love
i have for you out
there in the universe.

just to assure you
that it's never ending
and always expending.

i extract so much joy by simply
acknowledging you in my presence.

there's something magical about you
i can't seem to put into words just yet

and i'm not sure if i ever will.

you're a feeling that needs to be felt.
an experience which needs to be lived.

127

i know life is a dream because you're in it.

have you
ever heard
both sides
of the story

and they
were both
beautiful?

me and you
are like the

sunrise & sunset.

love languages change.

we won't always be able
to speak each other's fluently.

i teach you about mine.
you teach me about yours.

the journey never ends.

the universe could
separate us today

and i'd remain satisfied
for the rest of my life

remembering you.

131

time doesn't
exist when

i'm dwelling
in your divinity.

NAKED

no clothes.
no jewelry.
no make up.

naked.

no fear.
no guilt.
no shame.

naked.

no worries.
no thoughts.
no distractions.

naked.

no mind.
no body.
just spirit.

naked.

i know that at any given point
you could just flap your wings
and fly right back to heaven.

thank you for putting up with me.

talking to you late at night
is like talking to a mirror.

how selfish.
how beautiful.

we talk about the universe
and all the magic within it.

sometimes we forget that we're
talking about ourselves all along.

how selfish.
how beautiful.

- one consciousness

sure, the first kiss will
always remain special

but tomorrow's not promised.

that's why it's the last one
i don't ever want to forget.

being able to
witness you grow
over the years
has been an honor.

out of all the things
i could be proud of,
this is by far the one
i'm most proud of.

i'm proud of you.

your past self
wouldn't recognize
you today and i think

that's a beautiful thing.

my cheat code was having

you always believing in me.

OCEAN VIEW

you and the beach.
what a beautiful combination.

you and the waves.
what a beautiful illustration.

you and the ocean.
what a beautiful manifestation.

you and nature.
what a beautiful creation.

every day
i look at you
like i have just
seen the sky
change colors

for the first time.

MAGIC

i don't care what they
taught you in school.

2 me you are the
center of the universe.

2 me the sun is orbiting you.

2 me you are the pulling force
keeping this world in tact.

2 me you are living proof that
magic is not fiction but real in fact.

you are the most
beautiful thing
the universe decided
to manifest itself in.

<table>
<tr><td>if love</td><td>is</td><td>the art</td></tr>
<tr><td>thoughts</td><td>move</td><td>the paintbrush</td></tr>
<tr><td>feelings</td><td>embody</td><td>the colors</td></tr>
<tr><td>the world</td><td>represents</td><td>the canvas</td></tr>
<tr><td>and</td><td>i'm</td><td>the artist</td></tr>
</table>

then you're the painting.

the older i get

the more
i understand
what a
perfectly shaped
puzzle piece
you were and

continue to be.

145

we're just
two found souls
in the midst of the
great awakening.

what a time to be alive.

i saw you fearless.
i saw you scared.

i saw you smiling.
i saw you crying.

i saw you celebrating.
i saw you grieving.

i saw you at your best.
i saw you at your worst.

my perception of you
hasn't changed once.

to me you remain beautiful
no matter what life does to you.

147

i thank
the universe
for you by
loving you
the way
it loves me.

unconditionally.

the best thing i ever did

was learning to trust you.

149

i dream of
growing grey
together and
showing you

this page.

whenever i talk about love
i start describing you

and i don't even notice
changing the topic

but then again, i didn't.

you are the purest
form of poetry
i have ever seen.

no words out there
are put as well
together as you are.

152

our "what could've been"
would've followed me
for the rest of my life
like a shadow.

even the sunniest days
would've reminded me of you.

153

i don't know how much time i got left.

i just know i want to spend it with you.

154

flowers for you.

not because
you want them

but because
you deserve them.

NURTURING

mature enough to
plant our seeds
within ourselves and
not in each other.

we take care of
ourselves but never
hesitate to ask when
in need for water.

you help me, i support you.
we grow together.
sun out or dark clouds
we never mind the weather.

your worthiness is not a variable.
it can't be changed.

you're infinitely loved.

not by just me
but by the entire universe itself.

157

if this wasn't our
last visit on earth

i hope to reunite
with you once again

when this is all over.

i love how the silence
we share isn't filled with
awkwardness but wisdom.

we both can't help but smile
when we look at each other.

one conscious being
experiencing another one.

and when i run out
of words to say,

i hope you will still
look at me the same.

i hope to have said enough
for you to realize that

it's you whom i adore
and admire the most.

it has always been you.

i want to express my deepest gratitude
for making it this far.

thank you for dedicating your time
to read this collection.

truthfully,
matthew lovehall

about the author

matthew lovehall is simply
an extension and temporary
expression of the divine source
from where the entire
universe originates from.

socials

@matthewlovehall

www.matthewlovehall.com

Printed by BoD™in Norderstedt, Germany